GET
IT
DONE

A MEMOIR

VMH ™ Publishing
3355 Lenox Rd. NE Suite 750
Atlanta, GA 30326
www.vmhpublishing.com

The publisher is not responsible for websites, or social media pages (or their content) related to this publication, that are not owned by the publisher. Quantity sales. Special discounts are available on quantity purchases by corporations, associations, and others. For details, contact the publisher via email at: info@vmhpublishing.com

Obie Garrison Cover Photography: Vikki Jones
Paperback ISBN: 979-8-9853349-4-4
Ebook ISBN: 979-8-9853349-5-1

Library of Congress Control Number Available Upon Request

Published in United States of America

10 9 8 7 6 5 4 3 2 1

GET
IT
DONE

A MEMOIR

OBIE GARRISON

If you have a strong, positive self-image,
the effect will be that you will create and
attract more positive energy. This is hard to
manage and, if off-balance, can cause issues
that are difficult to navigate. The answer
to being out of your equilibrium is to pause,
take a moment and keep moving forward.

CONTENTS

INTRODUCTION

The most interesting subject offered in acquiring what we most desire is the development of self-discipline. In many cases, this will affect a person's capacity to enable character development, and this behavior will determine the outcome of our guidelines. The opportunity to advance is often involving both bravery and risk. In the end, there is nothing that can take the place of experience. Social influences are the process by which the presence or action of others modifies the behavior and constellation of opportunities. Your own ability to pursue the goals you seek can lead to abundance. The abilities we use to influence others are within each and every individual because we all use the method of reciprocity and assume that this method is a successful way to obtain return favors.

The action we use is a gamble, like most common behaviors in business, games, relationships, and authority. We are able to extrapolate from previous settings. This ability involves the idea of using credibility as a tool, useful in the notion of trust. It is a skill that is only achieved through perceived experience, attractiveness, and knowledge. A wise start to become a high achiever is implementing the love of taking a chance with a small amount of ambition. Ignoring this decision would be to miss out on a valuable instinct common in most people. We won't be rewarded every time because sometimes our judgment may be affected by persistent procrastination. This is the enemy of all humanity.

Our business is to choose which of the plans we decide to use to make a liberal profit for oneself from the investment term be recognized the behavior of the escort share prices. In ancient times, this was known as a "goddess of good luck," or the attraction of favorable attention in the hearts of man. Is there evidence of good fortune as a factor in the success of the world's richest and most powerful, or is it even common in all honest trades? Our country recently has been a witness to this strange effect that arose during the 2016 election year. Let's be honest; even the U.S. has never been given the occupants of the leading office without the courtship of some whimsical goddess.

Considering the wagers placed upon unpredictable events, we sometimes cast bets on which side we will hopefully be uppermost valuable. In a different light, escaping from the overlook of frequent events, suppose we consider it not to be natural to appreciate the assist of success without the generosity of perhaps a goddess. I subscribe to the idea that "to attract good things to oneself, it is necessary to take advantage of opportunities."

I also believe we are stubborn and often drive away opportunities by not accepting them. There are many examples of opportunities that become lost because of a failed action that was required. In fact, good fortune and success are not difficult to achieve once understood.

I SOLD MY HOUSE

The 2008 great recession was a period of marked general decline. This was observed globally in all national economies. Unemployment reported a record high of 10% at the beginning of the new White House administration. Collapse of the housing market was fueled by many financial indices: low-interest rates, easy credit, insufficient regulation, and toxic subprime mortgages. All these factors led to the economic crisis. Around this time, I graduated from High School, excited to begin my journey to pursue a college degree in engineering. I was moving from a small quiet town of Greenville, South Carolina, to the large and busy city of Atlanta. I remember as a child visiting Atlanta quite often with friends and family, but this time was different. I was now entirely out on my own and responsible for my own decisions. I lived with my cousins on campus for a while, then after a few semesters into college life, decided that living with relatives and going back and forth on campus was not something I wanted. Instead, I chose to live off-campus and manage a full-time school schedule and a job to support myself and my family.

I had savings for a rainy day at this time, a lesson in preparedness instilled in me at an early age by my mother. My plan was to go against the odds and develop ownership in my investments. With my frugality and savings, I had positioned myself to capitalize on the bursting of the U.S. housing bubble and the global financial crisis. My college professors helped me formulate this idea. In college, my history and political professors continuously lectured the class about the timing of the 2008 crisis. We now had a first black President. Overall, the country was experiencing what had to be compared to the Great Depression. From a historical perspective, history was repeating itself. In 2015, coming out of that financial crisis, all around the south and specifically Georgia, there were also an abundance of real estate foreclosures, short sales, evictions, and bank-owned properties.

I closed my first short sale deal on a real estate property before my twenty-fifth birthday. The property was bank-owned, and they wanted less than half of its estimated market value. It was a good deal and a potentially profitable investment opportunity. The decision was spurred on by the fact that I hated paying a monthly lease, so I literally jumped at the idea of ownership. The success of closing a short sale deal rather than a traditional thirty-day close fortunately lead to more opportunities. With larger equity I was able to take on more significant and lucrative business deals later on.

I encourage anyone with a need to invest to consider owning real estate. It is an easy decision to make, although it does require both discipline and commitment. The process from start to finish takes a year. The study of financial history has always appealed to me. In college, the history professors would always preach that history repeats itself, a theory that kept me engaged in the subject matter. This idea encouraged me to become more curious about the untold histories of our country: topics and events throughout our society that aren't usually discussed. There have been extreme events occurring in the U.S. dating back to 1918, often ten years apart. There is also a pattern to global events of this kind, occurring at intervals of one hundred years. Our generation has witnessed the milestones of pandemics, wars, and other crises. All have financial repercussions. Unfortunately, some people win, and some people lose in battles that are based on the economy. I encourage everyone to be on the winning side of the financial battle as often as possible and in any given situation.

The 2020 pandemic was a massive financial event that I had to get prepared for personally and professionally. In the reality of such a major event with vast financial effects world-wide, you can be as prepared as is possible yet still need to pivot and adapt to an unfamiliar environment. The housing market transformations due to the pandemic are no different from the 2008 great recession. Interest rates are at an all-time low, and the demand in the housing market has decreased, driving the prices of homes to record highs. Properties across the U.S. have increased in value, giving homeowners the option to sell at an elevated value to beat the economic bubble. Many homes had to try to deal with the full-blown financial crises caused by loss of jobs and illness.

I encourage anyone with a need to invest to consider owning real estate. It is an easy decision to make, although it does require both discipline and commitment.

BLACKOUTS

Great people have both great character and excellent abilities. Having one without the other is dangerous and can lead to obstacles that will damage one's physical health. We see this phenomenon often in those performing at high levels of creativity. In many cases, these episodes are ignored but they are often fatal to those we think highly of and cherish. You know the saying, "It happens to the best of us." I believe it. A catastrophic crash comes out of nowhere like a brick wall falling on you: smash. I see character to be the truth in who we are and our commitment to the mission we are accomplishing. That part of us makes us behave in a particular way in social situations, for example, friendly, unfriendly, confident, shy, honest, or dishonest. The world we live in requires us to match our capabilities with our character. Our talents as humans compete with both power and our ability to do something that tests the existence of why we are here. The discovery of our individual abilities is an everyday challenge. We learn how to handle complex issues on many levels, a feature shared by parents, comedians, entertainers, and athletes, to name a few. Each level of growth comes with an unspecified amount of pressure, pressure that is in the moment surprisingly unidentified.

In my experience, I can only testify to the transformation as coming from a higher power. African American people have been proof of these well-known circumstances and the ability to bounce back from catastrophic events throughout history. Unfortunately, tragedy does occur and cause devastation to people, countries, and in our lifetime, globally. Catastrophic events affect everything and everyone. They occasionally happen decades apart. Why? Suppose organizations are the cause of these events; simply put, a body of people, institutions and administrative companies that are the first to react, use the events for their particular purpose. The solution may be one in which the administration is given the power to gain control over the population and communities so that we are forced into survival mode. How do we deal with anxiety and fear? "We swim with sharks." We need to have such levels of intensity and refer to recovery as "the survival mode". We must be prepared. It is true that in a crisis, "You will go a lot further if you stop to refuel." The importance of knowing when to stop and refuel is very challenging. Unlike a car where the tank is either verified as full or empty, in an emergency the sustainable balance and perpetuation of routines are often the formula most of us use to power through. But what if you are doing all those right things consistently and performing logical operations? Is this enough? Good job! Pat yourself on the back, but you still need recovery. In this sense, I believe that the brick wall jumps out to stress us. Yes, we are doing well, both on a personal scale and at the global level, but the balance must be sustainable throughout the crisis.

My medical records report that I'm pretty healthy, with no significant history of family issues other than the obvious, so why do I experience blackouts? I can count on my hand the number of these episodes that occurred in my life and recall each in detail. My most recent blackout happened just months before the pandemic of 2020. I was deep into my performance routine and successfully building an array of audiences with my portfolio. I traveled across the country, networking and assembling clients within my corporation, doing what I love doing. One of many affirmations to occupy the day for me was:

> **"An active commitment to development fosters the confidence, focus, stamina, and mental agility to thrive and win."**

This formula I still use today. It covers tasks like highlights, emails, payrolls, missions, workouts, reading, meetings, team building, and holding myself accountable for a twenty-two-day game plan of running the business. Even though there is an average of thirty days each month, that period seemed too long to keep track of necessary operations. The game plan is to review and prepare for the upcoming month's plan on the twenty-second day. I was prepared. The office was firing on all cylinders, and the atmosphere in the room attested to the fact it was full of champions. Like any organization, conflicts of interest did occur, and I have a formula for that. We break down our issues, get to the root of the problem, and form solutions that favor the overall goal.

Simple, right? Operating simply is the mission of many and all successful corporations. Just ask

Elon Musk. And like those in any industry, we all encounter blackouts. All of us! It's a part of the game, much like the ice storm power outage that happened recently in 2020 in Texas. Is it a sign of evangelism? Whatever the belief is, this type of event is a message to regroup, innovate and redirect us to a new purpose. But the question I ask is, why does this happen at the expense of lives? We've all witnessed many innocent lives being lost with these pandemics and blackouts, and I did find myself involved in the immediate overload of having to manage through the crises. Both family and work are vital to me, and I was faced with the possibility of losing both by not having balance in myself. Even though I was in a state of readiness, the chance of losing both still happened. There is a saying: "The choices we make come with consequences." Okay. So, how can people do what they love without compromising their health and their relationships?

My advice is to be constantly prepared and always aware of your surroundings, just as I have been conscious enough in my episodes of blackouts. This seems easy to say but it is not exactly as simple as it sounds. I have beliefs: "Leadership cannot just go along to get along." and also "Leadership must meet the moral challenge of the day." At the critical moment, I made a list of actions I needed to do to accomplish my goals, hitting every mark. I had to take control because I had a conference coming up and I was tremendously excited about the new list of potential clients in the pipeline. The team was accelerating, and I was thrilled to meet what was next to come. The day was challenging as usual, but nothing out of the ordinary unmanageable- just standard business.

How much more effective can you be when everything is noted and aligned? I offered perspectives with my board of leaders sharing each other's ideas for the upcoming year. I believe the question was, "What do you predict will happen in 2020," or something like that? Chaos! The room went silent, "but manageable!" Now, this is on a corporate level, and from a general perception, every organization deals with business in quarters. It was in the heat of the fourth quarter. Manageable chaos is what we are built to overcome, so getting out of the red is, I believe, the term most used.

Cut down on expenses and capitalize on profitable opportunities. Remember when I said one without the other could be dangerous? Smack! I'm not exactly the history buff, but I know all caterpillars make cocoons before turning into butterflies, and flight school does not hatch any shortcomings. My gut feeling knew something big was on the future horizon. Still, I never thought it would be known as a symbiotic relationship; I had been introduced to a well-qualified candidate that came out of nowhere. Whether it's long-term, mutualistic, or commensalism, these relationships have created and built our country. To who's benefit across allies, you can probably guess correctly.

Unannounced but prepared for opportunity, my second blackout hit me. It seemed to have come back-to-back. Without revealing myself to the new candidate, we conducted a conversation with professionalism. The candidate was open-minded and thrilled to seek a new challenging adventure, but her health was a serious issue. I would have never understood the challenges of a more deserving candidate if I had not been honest with her from the first handshake. The candidate mentioned that she had a condition with night vision blindness. As a result, she is unable to drive after dusk. I was taken aback. What? She said that she rarely tells a single person outside of her family and close friends. "That's good to know. Sorry to hear that, but why do you hide such important information?" I don't think I asked her this way, but I was in recovery mode myself. She explained that I made her feel that she wanted to be involved in the organization, and the opportunity was promising. True, I thought, but "Why?" was the thought running through my head. She then let me know that I was continuously rubbing my eyes and drying my tears. This made her feel comfortable talking about herself more. In one of my most vulnerable states, I had tried my best to display both character and capabilities. I had felt no physical pain other than being mortal and had trusted myself without judgment or fear of reaction towards completing a mission. I had to reflect on myself and understand how blessed I am to have overcome my situation at that moment.

Unannounced but prepared for opportunity, my second blackout hit me. How much more effective can you be when everything is noted and aligned?

FATHERHOOD

My relationship with my son is, in my opinion, adventurous. We are defined as opposite personalities, which for me, is a good thing. For example, he is very outgoing and will fill a room with small talk-talk that may eventually lead to more communication revealing how smart and knowledgeable he is. My view of communication is more subtle. Mine is low-key, and I like to feel the energy of the environment before speaking. I enjoy this approach with the relationship I have with my son. It helps me to use clever and indirect methods to analyze his learning and development curve.

He likes sports of many kinds, football, soccer, and to my surprise, he is excellent at board games like chess and monopoly. I like motorsports, race cars, motorcycles, and pretty much anything dealing with speed and acceleration. A troubling issue is that my son can't tolerate loud noises as much as I can, but we are able to compromise and enjoy each other's sports endeavors. Being a father is the best thing that ever happened to me. Since day one, I have enjoyed the ride. It hasn't been at all easy. I believe any parent would agree this to be true. The true aspiration for me is that I have always wanted to have a son. When I first learned it was a boy, I was excited and thrilled to have a mini-me running around this world, and for the most part, I wouldn't change a thing. Having my son means so much to me, and I am truly grateful and blessed. Being a father to my son has evolved as I assumed the responsibility of raising a boy to becoming a man. These changes, I believe, come from a daily learning cycle. We both learn as we together deal with each of the challenges and issues of life. The tasks can be demanding but well worth the investment. With this responsible process, I have learned to be more patient. This means understanding that my son is a child, and I am the adult, so what I say, and mean is coming from the heart but is authoritative. So, I needed to learn when to be serious and when to be playful and how to set the required boundaries- the same as between man to man, this concept continues in the relationship between adult and child. On a day-to-day basis, for example, I must make sure my son's schoolwork is completed and correct and ready for the next day. I also have to make sure he has proper hygiene and eats healthily.

I also need to understand how his day went. I have learned that kids go through things too, just like adults, but I have been surprised on many occasions by what I learn when simply asking," How did your day go today?" I want my son to trust me enough to share real situations with me and not be afraid to hide any topic of concern or excitement. My son's successes are my successes, and when he knows that he can be comfortable with sharing information with me, I feel it is truly relationship building between father and son. The most fundamental part of communication is trust. My plan for his success is that for whatever he wants or chooses to be in life, he able to understand the platform needed for him to succeed, whether football or innovative technology. I unfold my plan for him by providing opportunities for my son to think for himself with whatever interest he chooses and whatever pressure he may encounter. That way, if he does decide to move forward with whatever he is interested in, it's because he wants to invest that amount of time .I have found this to be satisfying for both of us to understand a least three of his personalities by allowing him to be himself at times. I have learned a few of his strengths and weakness characteristic traits from listening and observing him alone. He can be a bit of a spoiled whiney individual when things aren't going his way, even though he is putting in a reasonable effort. What I am most proud of is his ability to not give up on himself. I discovered this in his early stages of learning, from potty training to first bike fall to catching long football passes; he's not afraid to fail and willing to keep trying. My advice to other fathers is to take it one day at a time and to embrace each experience spent with our children, which is the opportunity to show love.

My advice to other fathers is to take it one day at a time and to embrace each experience spent with our children, which is the opportunity to show love.

WHAT HAPPENED

I want to start by giving an understanding of what benefits there are in working in corporate America -from developing leadership skills and life skills. One should work towards leadership development to become more aware of how people are in this world and build a communication skill set. The environment in the workplace should start with this standard: the bar is extremely high and volatile for equality with anyone on board and joining the creative organization space. The core values are established with meaning and a purposeful-driven life many can and want to acquire. Whether one wants to create a business plan for life or a road map to create a vision of self-sufficient linguistics fresh from scratch to take on the world, it starts with one question. The gem in this chapter has a more significant impact on my life than I would have ever guessed.

I have discovered many principles. These have evolved from interactions with influential people to every day you and me people, to I can't believe I'm standing in front of this person. Still, I never thought I could learn an essential principle of love in a million years. What does it mean? Can you see it? Can you feel it? Here are a few shares that I've picked up along the way.

#1: The purpose of life is to love and be loved, in that order. Every shot counts in this image because it is a reflection of self. I don't mean this in an arrogant or egotistical way, but in a secure and fulfilling way. I have learned that many of us can't say "I love you" to ourselves. You must love yourself before you can indeed have the capacity to love others is a whole mouth full. Saying it is not the hard part; believing it is life changing.

#2: To serve is to live. Okay.

#3: It is nice to be necessary, but it is more important to be nice. Got it.

I was aligned in a position where I had no idea what, why, or how to navigate the golden circle. I do believe some leaders lead, and a cause or purpose drives those. At the time, my job was to discover purpose. Whether it was a need or want, how does this make sense to you? That's easy, right? "How" has a lot to do with feeling, textures, notions, you know, the physical aspect of something? For example, I know I need this because it helps with my sleeping habits. How about I want this because it brings out the empirical definition of my hair. These are the fundamentals of how anyone can succeed in the market.

If you can discover the need and want in people, you can define your demand value. There is more on "How", but the "What" has a lot to deal with language. People don't buy into "what" you do. They buy into "why" you do it. From my experience, when you've personally undergone, encountered, or lived through something, your voice can give anecdotal narrative to your account which claims truth and meaning. What can we control in our opportunity? This question is relevant in every human being's language. Whether you're bi-lingual or not, energy is evident in the developmental path to our future selves. Where do you see yourself in the future? I got the chance to ask this question so many times to so many people I believe I've said it in my sleep, sources say.

The events that happen in our lives are undetected, unplanned, off-balance, and in times, problematic. I called this the "Event" stage in life. Like myself, I'm sure you have had an event that took an unexpected turn in your life due to no fault of your own. Maybe you have known someone with the experience. The question always has come back to the idea of control for me. I need to know if I am in control of a situation. I've spent years not understanding that this is a simple 'yes' or 'no' answer. When the answer is "No," I know for a fact only God himself can handle it. "Who am I to fix that?" I say to myself now. Often I can't help myself, and try to take control. It sounds crazy, I know, but I have lived by the axiom, if I can help, then I will help for a very long time. Although I have no regrets about this, I know this can only be beneficial through self-love.

Going back to #2, To serve is to live. One may say you can take this to account for any person serving our very country. True, but I find it difficult to wrap my head around the fact that many of our American troops have fought and died for reasons created by none other than the egotistical narcissist.

That same concept interestingly creeps into our minds in the professional work environment. It is said that politics and religion should not uphold or consider courtship in the professional space, but how can this be when our country, hell, this universe, engage in such premises. For example, the government or some churches are established businesses, right? Maybe this is just me. I was forced to face reality when it came to others' perspectives, motives, and goals.

What tremendously helped me understand an effortless but immense silence that undergoes choosing your adventures in life is asking ourselves, "Who are you?" Don't ever forget that. Schools, jobs, bosses, family and friends, even places play a significant role in this competence ladder.

Developing awareness in your skill levels requires different emotions at different stages of the learning process. Particularly subject to self-doubt, the Dunning-Kruger effect, and in many cases, there is the manipulation to try to maneuver us to betray ourselves.

"Corporate America cannot claim to speak for Black America without working to empower Black leaders." a recent tweet by Robert F. Smith. As a result of the conscious matrix, small doses of pain are recognized by the fourfold path.

"What is one's hustle?" This is one more of many questions I got the opportunity to ask many people. With #3, I've used the outside/inside hustle with a high degree of success to simplify relationships when dealing with people in different cultures and to evolve in diverse stages of development. What was evident to me was the efficiency of the these four paths in helping me to develop teams. This picture later came as a bite of reality. In the beginning, we may not realize how much we need to learn, then we discover what we don't know. I called this "the reaction stage in life." Most situations go two ways, good and bad. How you approach them directly generates collaborations with predictability and repeatability routes. Okay, so the outside/inside hustle was getting a foot in the door in any situation. But the movement towards getting yourself to the upside hustle requires more unidirectional movement. There are up, down, and sideways routes, all ultimately pulling you away from what you are, to what you will become. For example, you can become a Black Leader. I'm not against any ethnicity or social group. I challenged myself with everyone. To me, this was my power move. It works, and just like getting that foot in the door, proving your value and earning your promotion is what gets me up each day. Inside and outside of these waters is developing creative achievements not just for one, but for all. I learned the hard way, how can we break the mold of what it means to be a modern leader? Recognizing how we feel in each stage of learning helps us stay focused and manage all of the emotional ups and downs on the path to leadership goals.

"So, how did I get here?" I ask myself. I was hustling. I had differentiated from the rest of the pack to set the stage for the opportunity of a lifetime. Writing, planning, content programming, marketing, designing, taking phone calls, whatever else requires us to do the little things each day most people won't. I cared about cultivating talent from within and developing loyal teams bound to success. What I learned from this plight was why I desire to create a context of opportunity for others to share and celebrate the future with me. Paying it forward was one of many achievements that came with my accomplishments. Still, I don't think we as a culture have seen enough of it in today's world. Black leaders, Women leaders, people of color all deserve equal opportunity. Those doors should not be closed based on gender or skin color. In reality, our success depends on how well we manage the reactions we are faced with to control those outcomes we want.

I am in charge of "why" because the difference I make today leads to a better tomorrow.

If you can discover the need and want in people, you can define your demand value. What tremendously helped me understand an effortless but immense silence that undergoes choosing your adventures in life is asking ourselves, "Who are you?" Don't ever forget that.

5

TIME RUNNING OUT

Too often, I've been in the presence of eliciting moments. Whether good or bad, the extracted lessons learned will be something to remember and if good, keep using over time. Failure to be noticed or remembered has always been a process to which allows me to go inside myself. The subject matter is always tense to resonate around the passing of a close or loved one. Ever since I was young, I remember gravitating to reverberating sounds that rattle walls, like thunder striking when pouring rain out. Up until I was about nine years old, I had experienced episodes of ear infections. It seemed like they never stopped coming back, one after another, and they would last for about two weeks. No doctor, emergency room, or parent could help resolve the pain. I had to sit there and feel every thump. Hearing the rattles of my head and the pressure of my pulse for days on end, a pain I wouldn't wish upon anyone, made me want to pull my ears off my head.

As I think back, these were the moments that helped me become a calmer person. There was no cure, and I had no choice but to endure the pain could have been a factor. I had built up a tolerance not for the pain because I am not the strong one in this fight when handling pain levels, but for the measurements when they occur. I had gotten so used to them frequently, and I could feel when an episode was coming. Sort of like when you can tell you was getting sick as the seasons change, but I felt fine. My temperature was a little high, looked normal.

The only difference was my ears were on fire. It was hard to communicate with any friends because, for one, I couldn't nearly hear them, and two, I couldn't hear myself, and three, it was a pain I couldn't explain and that no one could physically see. Mostly I was quiet and kept to myself. I kept track of the timing between each thump. It was my heartbeat. I'm no doctor, but to keep my mind off the pain, I kept track of those taps: Tap-tap, tap-tap, tap-tap, that kind of rhythm. But a rhythm of pain to come with it. They would slow down and speed up as I tried to play around to forget it or get louder as I forced myself to ignore them while sleeping.

The noises were heard either way. At the time, I didn't appreciate them as much as I realized I should. After a few years, finally, something was available to help me. I had gotten tubes put into my ears, a surgery I had to undergo, and I remember till this day how they put me to sleep. I was given a choice, chocolate or bubble gum. I chose gum, and I remember the colors and smell of the room, and the feeling of my ears popping like I was going through the mountains, then it was lights out. When I woke up, I had no more pain.

It wasn't until around age eleven or twelve that I realized that I hadn't had any ear infections as often as in the past. I still had the feelings and the tasteless smells of when I knew one was coming back in either one or both ears. Still, the episodes were shortened to about a day or two and would disappear. I had gotten used to looking forward to counting the time it would take for the pain to go away. On my thirteenth birthday, I remember all I wanted to do was celebrate not having ear infections. No presents or gifts of that nature made me happier than not having to deal with that pain. I remember losing one of my tubes during the summer, and I thought the world would end.

I felt my ears pop when I went swimming for the first time since having tubes put in my ears. I remember my mom said I couldn't go swimming, but the urge took over, and in I went. I thought she would be mad at me, and I would have another surgery to reinstall the tubes. I didn't say anything for a while. When it was time to visit the doctor, he said that one of my tubes had fallen out and had no pain from infections lately. I said no, and the doctor agreed that we didn't need to install anymore and that they did their job. I can't recall how the other one fell out, but that's when things started to turn. As any other kid my age believed, time wasn't something that had any value. We were just kids and teenagers growing up. Having been alone and able to hear and keep count of my pulse as much as I did as a kid helped me understand to value humanity as an adult. I had to hide a lot of my emotions as a kid to keep myself familiar amongst my family and friends because the pain made me want to bawl up and cry my face dry, and that has never been me coming up from my testosterone-driven uncles and brothers, get it together attitude.

I hadn't had much trouble from ear infections other than knowing when one was coming back as an adult. It's that awful moment that stops you in your tracks to get prepared for something tragic. Because I could measure out for about two weeks of pain as a kid, I pretty much knew when the time was running out, and things got back to normal. As an adult, strangely, the pain of ear infections was no longer a significant factor, the passing of someone I knew or was relatively close to crept surfacing around that beginning time.

Every time the feeling of having to endure that groggy pain came back, I started to notice myself present at funerals. The pain and those tap-tap, tap-tap, tap-tap would come back. I never really spoke up or told anyone about it. It was something I dreaded for years, but I was not sure why it was happening this way or whether it was/is a coincidence. I wanted to avoid every second of it, not attending funerals and certainly that pain coming back. The lessons I learned from listening to those taps and thumps in my head during my childhood somehow became a habit when dealing with situations the older I got. I learned just to listen and breathe to keep myself calm and de-escalate the extent. Nothing has changed the outcomes, and the times these two sequences occur. It's one of those times you prepare for and work through the best way possible, I say to myself.

I learned just to listen and breathe to keep myself calm and de-escalate the extent. Nothing has changed the outcomes, and the times these two sequences occur. It's one of those times you prepare for and work through the best way possible,

6

FUSION CAPITAL

Each of our personal success stories is a direct result of a unique way we adapt our ideas within our culture. Entrepreneurship is a way people can connect themselves to an extreme challenge or situation in the world. Most of the skill traits in many individuals relate to getting something done or improving and developing a solution to a problem. Whatever the case or process, principled innovation makes things more accessible for people to operate and believe in. Systems, codes, products, and services are a few major industries that make up the overall mindset we all strive to achieve our goals. Fusion Capital was founded upon those same principles and morals.

Growing up, I did well in school, my grades were good, and sports were a big part of my family, like football, basketball, and track.

I remember playing ball in middle school at the gym, shooting around the court with my friends getting ready for tryouts. I didn't have much interest in basketball like my friend did. I would say I was a tag-along to put my best forward to see if I could make the team. While playing intensely, dribbling the ball down the court, I noticed a sharp pinch in my right hand. I didn't think about it at the time and kept progressing to make my lay-up drill. It wasn't until the next pass from my team ate that I realized I could not grip the ball. Instant pain hit the nerves of my right pinky, and I noticed as I looked down, it didn't look normal. I couldn't move it at all. "Is it broken?" I asked myself. "No way, how can you break a finger dribbling a ball?" Indeed, it was broken. My friends went on to try out for and make the team. On the other hand, I was horsing around to help my friend prepare for tryouts and ended up with an injured hand for a month and a half. I didn't appreciate basketball after that incident for a while.

I had always had an independent mind when it came to taking care of myself and sitting out and watching my friends who made the team play, so I decided to earn some money for myself by cutting grass. I would earn fifty dollars a yard and averaged about 3 to 4 a week during the school year. That was when my love for entrepreneurs first began. I liked the idea of hustling for yourself and creating an income at an early age, and that edge grew as I got older and more educated. I've always known that owning your own company would benefit not only yourself but the people around you and can make a difference.

I'd constantly seek out new clients and find creative ways to earn money in addition to cutting grass. That was the foundation to building the morals and values of running a business that people can be proud of and respect. Today, Fusion Capital is an engaged partner in collaborating with management teams and shareholders by leveraging commercial industrial and residential property operations. Whether the client is a start-up or has been established in operation for years like Bissell, our team drives innovation and investments to increase production. After discovering a large interruption gap in diversity within specific industries involving the retail, real estate, finance, and technology sectors, the idea started. Being a Chief Executive in target markets with favorable demographic fundamentals for medium and long-term growth is not shared amongst minority and significant community development.

An average of 1% of Board seats at private companies is backed by top U.S. venture and private equity firms. The goal of operations is to bridge the gap and educate on having access to equity capital in high-performance organizations. Just like the lessons learned when I was trying different sports and activities to discover a purpose in life, this business has ups and downs. There is no straight road to success, and there will be some bumps and bruises. My advice is to become aware of the bumps and to consistently commit to being a student of your environment and have a meaningful application to the work you are pursuing.

Consistently commit to being a student of your environment and have a meaningful application to the work you are pursuing.

COMFORT ZONES

I have many examples to discuss with understanding personality, comfort zones, and managing your introvert or extrovert performance. I want to start using the build from the ground-up approach to explain the learning curve and how anyone can go from good to great. Early on in my development, I was unaware of whether I was an extrovert or introvert nor had a clue of knowing how to recognize the trait in myself, let alone anyone else. To grow in any industry or profession requires being hands-on, studying the game, and applying feedback. I was conscious enough to understand getting outside of my comfort zone from a phycological point of view. I knew I had to throw myself in the ring and be prepared for anything to happen to beat the intensiveness of that turtle in a shell I have been used to. I was able to find contentment at a low level, and my hopes are you will too.

For a long time, I've used formulas to make things simpler in life, and the one that helped me the most is KSE: Knowledge, Strategy, Execution. With that being said, I had to gather the data of knowing how to perform. So where does one gather that information? Sports. Who is the greatest of all time, in your opinion? Think about that question. I called this, "adapt the personality of others". The make and model of who you want to be can easily come from entitled unreal expectations. Most people stay in place, and this causes them not to believe that someone owes them anything. You owe it to yourself to invest the time and to challenge your humility. What are the excuses? There are none. I started with "The Make": how the person looks, the image/character and instincts. "The Model": this is the viewpoint on mentality, ambition, work ethic, and also successes achieved. You're probably not going to like what I say, but emotions and anxiety will kill you faster than a bullet. I had to learn to be consistent and manage my emotional intelligence. I have been good at this in life. Still, I wanted to challenge myself professionally and believe that I could get better and grow. So, here I was in the moment with people I had never seen before in my life, and they were as anxious and as a crowd of consumer war vets on Black Friday.

Imagine an unknown number of grown infants screaming at the top of their lungs for milk on demand. Okay, imagine how your heart stopped when you first found out that our new president of the United States of America was Barack Obama. Times have changed for the history of our country. Yes, this was the perfect time to take control of my situation.

Negative outlooks can be devastating in most ordinary circumstances, but I was not about to fail. I understood the idea of levels of leadership and was fully aware at which level I had been dealing with throughout my time. The position was the entry-level, I remembered, and the learning curve was already established. I was addressing an audience. Then chaos broke loose. There was no one else to control the situation, and my compensation was at stake. I had to believe in myself to control the situation. The position I was in had been established, and everyone already knew who was in charge. When I think back to my mistake, this reenactment turned it into an 'aha' moment. But that was nothing to think about in that moment. Luckily, there was one person in the charge of remuneration that was on my side-he knew. I remembered I was able to set the tone of the meeting from the beginning, and the engagement of my fundamentals was working well. Somehow the surprise was revealed before my intentions, and the impulse increased from level three to twenty-three. Wow, what a good thing, right? Wrong. A good thing is only good if you can use discipline; otherwise, you will retain inherent chaos and confusion.

I had built that audience by following my fundamentals. The new onlookers had to know what was going on. They just liked what they saw. I had to keep going with what I had and take advantage of what had to come. I could relate to this theory by understanding that the most successful people are not those with the best swing but those who just get up to bat the most. I had to close the deal. Not only the deal with my existing audience, but with the unaware intensive information-seeking members too. I had to start over. Not everyone wants to start over, and not everyone wants to continue after or during chaotic situations. I made the wise decision with the help of the lucky individual who was on my side earlier. I kept the engagement going so well, and my existing audience was with me allowing me to be patient and calm. The entire meeting understood what was going on and how everyone could benefit. This only lasted for a few seconds. Let's face it, people want things now and fast, and by this time, the surprise was out of the box and well out in the open. So what do you do? I had to start over again. From the beginning.

The question now is: "How do you move a crowd?" You speak, you're heard, you sustain the ability to focus on the overall goal. Once I introduced myself again, that broke the ice. I was able to invite, welcome, gather new listeners, and unveil my contract. Most common contracts are signed agreements, but in this case, there was no paper or pen. What I mean by unveiling my contract is giving people something to hold on to, a form of intention for something else to come. This contract reveal has no cost. It's free. It's who you are. Same as at your favorite rap artist concert when they bring out a special guest or have an artist open up for them, but when you are a performer, you yourself are the opening and the closing act. Without the first three fundamentals conducted correctly, there is no close. Before you can hustle, you must see things differently and tap into undercurrents to get things done faster. Focus on volume completion. I am only trying to save you from failure. You must be able to introduce yourself with authority and authentic confirmation.

I am, my name is, is a good start. Most important, it is to think for the life you want, not the life you currently have. The willful act of doing is our secret weapon. To be loyal to our hustle, we must be willing to betray our old self so that our new self can gain momentum. Never give up.

We must be willing to betray our old self so that our new self can gain momentum.

www.ingramcontent.com/pod-product-compliance
Lightning Source LLC
Chambersburg PA
CBHW021144130726
47988CB00003B/1456